I0183772

ePiphany

"Lessons from My Middle Aged Clarity"

TrubuPRESS is a subsidiary of the Trubu Media Group whose interests include but are not limited to fiction and non fiction stories from the black experience throughout the American and African Diaspora.

Publisher: TrubuPRESS
Editor: Neo Blaqness
Cover Design: TrubuPRESS
Proofreaders: Cynthia Utley, Tamika Coleman

EPIPHANY: Lessons from My Middle Aged Clarity
Copyright © 2013 Neo Blaqness

All rights reserved. No part of this book may be reproduced or transmitted in any form or by any means without written permission from the author. Permission is granted for brief excerpts to be published for book reviews .

To order NEO BLAQNESS: ePIPHANY
visit http://trubupress.com
or call (872) 22TRUBU

Booksellers:
Retail discounts are available from TrubuPRESS. Inquiries about volume orders can be made via the phone number listed above.

ISBN-13: 978-0615875415
ISBN-10: 0615875416
Published by TrubuPRESS

PRINTED IN THE UNITED STATES

DEDICATION
GLASS DARKLY

"Today I pause
That I might thank God
For the keepers
Of my heart
You precious few
Without whom
My life would be
Quite dark
The light you share
Tho you not dare
To think it to be so grand
Casts the Son
Upon each shadow
Of my inner man
You who see
Beyond the outward me
The man who has
Answered this call
And hold me up
So prayerfully

That I not tempt
The fall
From His grace
But face to face
Washed clean
Upon the sure
To view this life
Through Heaven's eyes
Glass darkly
Nevermore"

-Neo Blaqness-

CONTENTS

TABLE OF CONTENTS

TABLE OF CONTENTS

FOREWORD

IN THE FORM OF LETTER TO NEO

I am still amazed at all the projects you have going at one time. And yet you manage to keep them going while keeping your eyes on the prize. After hearing you read the excerpts from your book series, I began to see that is the same passion you bring to everything you do.

As I am reminded about the many facets of your life, I realize the common theme is the passion you bring in everything, including your ability to love.

You also have the audacity to invoke that same kind of passion that lay dormant within people and, most certainly, with whomever you're intimately involved.

At least this is how I feel. Passionate! I bet if I polled everyone who had, have, or will have the pleasure of interacting with you, each would come to the same conclusion:

You inspire, motivate and provoke people.

FOREWORD

Your goal is to dust off the minds of the human race and get us thinking. Not like you, but thinking, none the less. A mind is a terrible thing to waste and you refuse to let anyone do that on your watch.

I ask myself, how can one man care THAT much? I know I don't have the gift of words and I feel so inadequate trying to wrap my arms around how to tangibly describe you. Maybe that's the problem. One word to describe you... Ha! I've got to be kidding myself to think for one moment I can sum you up.

-Carolyn

INTRODUCTION

Many people go through a middle aged crisis. But, for me, I had a middle aged clarity. This book contains my personal epiphanies from it.

Far from a traditional thinker, I thought it best to start with the blunt objects before moving on to the more refined quotes and excerpts contained in these pages.

RACISM

is a tool of the rich to keep the poor fighting among themselves. Give the white man a darker man to blame while you are busy turning everyone into "niggers". That is the true lesson of political economics. There are no rich racists. The god of greed comes in all colors.

RELIGION

is the creation of the powerful to give the weak minded someone else to cry to other than their own divine sensibilities. There are no "Holy" books or "Holy" men- just holes in the truth filled by man's imagination and lust for power. Religion provides us an excuse to blame God or the Devil for our own irresponsible and lazy choices while hiding behind the foolishness of prophets and preaching.

GOD

is who we are. It is neither vain nor blasphemous to understand that, just as our sons and daughters were born to be us, that we were born to be as the Creator is. Life is not about eternal worship, but constant growth- which is not about blessings, but understanding the way, the truth, and the life of what we were created to be. As such, none of us is called above any other. We rise according to our own desire for wisdom, and in equal fellowship share in what we know.

SEX

without love is just like taking morphine when there is no pain- just another addiction for losers with dead end lives. Sharing body parts like dirty needles and rolling the dice with each injection. Passion without

INTRODUCTION

love is lust- just another deed done for self-ish reasons. But a passionate love creates intimacy with a need and desire to know and to share and to empower one another spirit-ually, physically, and emotionally.

MONOGAMY

as a form of righteousness is a myth- a creation of the hypocrite to cover their lusts, and a security blanket of the abused to cov-er their pain and jealousy. Who we love and how we love is not about numbers, it is about honesty and choice.

LOVE

is the only reason we live this life. It is what we are here to learn and the only way we can be trusted with the power and re-sponsibilities of our spiritual nature when we leave this place. Without love we cannot be god with God and must be separated to another place where we can do no harm for however long it takes for us to learn to love. That is the true nature of Hell- the distance and separation of us from the Creator.

TRUTH

is what we choose to see for ourselves

and not what others say it is. It cannot be seen through fear or intimidation, nor through promises of acceptance, love, or heavenly reward. It must stand alone in the coldness of unrepentant scrutiny, ignorance, even mockery- fearing no blasphemy; neither lashing out in its defense. For it is not a physical thing to be covered or diminished, as it cannot be removed from ones heart.

These are my truths. Lessons from My Middle Aged Clarity. You are entitled to disagree and believe otherwise. But what is more important is that you find your own reasons for what you believe, and live honestly in it. *-Neo Blaqness-*

ePiphany

"Lessons from My Middle Aged Clarity"

By Neo Blaqness

———————

TRUBU PRESS

A Black Legacy Publishing Company

Epiphany*

Syllabification: (e·piph·a·ny)
Pronunciation: /iˈpifənē/

noun (plural epiphanies)

(also Epiphany)
the manifestation of Christ to the Gentiles as represented by the
Magi (Matthew 2:1-12).

- the festival commemorating the Epiphany on January 6.
- a manifestation of a divine or supernatural being.
- a moment of sudden revelation or insight.

from the Oxford Dictionary

FREE LOVE

"**A** heart that is won is never as valuable as one freely given."

-Neo Blaqness-

DEAF

"The greatest truths about ourselves are often found in our reasons for not wanting to hear it.**"**

-Neo Blaqness-

ARSON

"A truth that you choose not to face, does not fail to exist simply because you turn your eyes from it. It will burn like an unattended wild fire until it ultimately consumes the forest of your life, forcing new growth from beneath the ash heap of your folly."

-Neo Blaqness-

LONG GONE

" **C**hoosing to live in the past is like praying to make it through a storm that everybody else already knows is over."

-Neo Blaqness-

WALKABOUT

"If you work really hard, one of the best and most influential persons in life you will ever have the pleasure of meeting, will be the undiscovered you."

-Neo Blaqness-

MR. GORBACHEV

"When your ears grow weary from the echoes of life, consider tearing down the walls which send back the sound."

-Neo Blaqness-

HESITATION

"Sometimes what is lost through hesitation can be more costly than taking a chance. It is always best to examine your reasons. When you know that something is wrong, then it is wise not to take a chance that things might be different when something inside is telling you to wait.

But if your hesitation is out of fear, and since we know that God did not give us a spirit of fear, then the choice to move forward is not really taking a chance, but is merely an opportunity that requires a leap of Faith. When you understand the difference, you will know how to better recognize the answers to your prayers."

-Neo Blaqness-

SOUNDING BRASS

" I have found in my life that the difference between a knowledgeable person and a wise person is that a knowledgeable person lives to prove he is right, while a wise person, more often, prays that he is wrong."

-Neo Blaqness-

A PERFECT FOOL

"Perfection is the ambition of a fool who does not know how to live. Grace is the walk of the wise who have learned how to love.**"**

-*Neo Blaqness*-

CLOUD DANCING

"Celebrating your success is a lot like mountain climbing. Because the air is so thin, you can't dance on top of a mountain until your body is used to being there. It is of little wonder why people who are quick to dance, so easily fall off the cliff."

-Neo Blaqness-

FAILURE

"The easiest failures to accept are when you know you did something wrong- because those are things you can fix. But when you know in your heart, that given another chance, you wouldn't do anything differently; despite what may seem to be lost as a result, much more has been gained. Your dignity."

-Neo Blaqness-

A FORGOTTEN POINT

"**W**hen you are young, they always remind you to never run with scissors. But when you are older, they forget to warn you about the grown ups running with daggers."

-Neo Blaqness-

PARUMPAPUMPUM

"**E**ven when you think you have nothing to give, you always have a prayer."

-Neo Blaqness-

THE REAPING

"A seed, whether deliberately planted or sown by the wind, does not change the fruit it was meant to bear."

-Neo Blaqness-

WANTED

"**T**he value of something desired, will never exceed the worth of having a true need fulfilled."

-Neo Blaqness-

SPEED BUMPS

"Today it seems we strive to be so much in love with ourselves, that we drive everywhere with our face in the mirror, complaining that someone needs to fix the bumpy road while clueless that those bumps are actually the people we are running over."

-Neo Blaqness-

THE TIES THAT BIND

" **A** person who feels the need to be minding your business, often sees more profit potential in your life than theirs. Be careful not to assume that it is always because they want something from you. Sometimes they just want something better FOR you. "

-Neo Blaqness-

OF SERVICE

"**B**ringing a smile to the humble minded is like a glass of cold water to the hard working. But to the vain, it is like a servant giving lemonade to the master floating on a pool of self importance."

-Neo Blaqness-

FOR NO GOOD REASON

"Someone who
makes you smile
for no good reason
is like someone
who can make you eat
when you ain't even hungry
There's just something
in the seasoning
Like salt on a sweet apple
somehow pulls out the flava
or crunching
through a hard shell
to the softness you savor
A smile is
the exhale of sadness
released like the laughter
of a sputtering balloon
when gladness un-knots
the stale air within

And that someone
who makes you smile
for no good reason
is the truest definition
of a friend"

-Neo Blaqness-

FRAGILE

"I was taking out the garbage today and I noticed that one of my neighbors, who recently bought one of the units, had thrown away a lot of boxes. One was a lamp box with the word fragile stamped on it in big letters.

Of course, I had seen plenty of boxes like that before, but something caught my attention this time around. I guess, as you grow older, simple things begin to have greater meaning, and I began to think about the word fragile.

The word on the box was a warning that what was inside could be easily broken. But when we use the same word about a person being fragile, it has a very different meaning. In my mind, a fragile person was usually someone who was weak. For whatever reason, you had to treat them with the proverbial kid gloves for fear of causing damage. I used to think that kind of person was, basically, punking out on life.

But I grew to learn that there are many reasons why a person could be in a "fragile state". However, unlike the sign on the box, the difference is that the lamp was actually made out of glass; people are not. People usually become fragile as a result of the actions of other people. That is not the same as becoming physically fragile due to age. I am talking about the point to which we can cause so much weight to bear on someone's heart and mind that we become responsible for crushing their spirit.

I cannot say that I have ever been truly fragile, but I have been close. But for the grace of God, and the love shown through some real friends.

The box was also marked fragile so that it would avoid being put in a place on the truck where it could be compressed by other boxes. Then the contents were wrapped to avoid any breakage from the box just bumping around.

In life, when we wrap our arms around someone, we call it compassion. We are protecting them from the compression of life. The only difference is, people are not expected to need that protection forever. Unlike the lamp, we are all capable of growing beyond a fragile state. But sometimes that requires a lot of protective arms taking turns while that person strengthens.

But when yours are the only arms protecting a fragile spirit, even when others appreciate what you have done, nobody notices what you had to absorb on behalf of that person. When that lamp box was opened, nobody asked the bubble wrap how was the ride. But it would have been called a worthless piece of crap if the lamp had been broken.

Compassion can be a thankless job sometimes because nobody counts all the things you did to protect someone– just the one thing you couldn't. You can't look for fault or blame. You can't accept guilt. Sometimes, that's just life." -*Neo Blagness*-

TIME OUT

"**K**nowing when it is time to stand back and let someone fall is not something that can be taught. It has to be felt. The best way I can put it is that when it comes to the point where your frustration and anger begins to stand in the way of the principle you are trying to get across, or when the friend begins to personalize everything you are trying to get them to see, or when every point you make is met with an excuse as to why something is not as bad as you are trying to get them to see, or if everything you say is twisted into reasons why you just want to get your way as though there is some great benefit to your taking over their life when you have enough to take on with your own, then it is time to step back. It is time to understand that you are standing in the way of the lesson. It is time

to let your silence speak for however long is
necessary."

-Neo Blaqness-

PROFIT CARING

"**D**o not invest more in people than they are willing to invest in themselves, unless you are willing to run their life for them while allowing them to keep all the profit."

-Neo Blaqness-

UNBECOMING

"**L**eaving someone where they choose to stay is not the same as leaving someone behind. Staying anyway out of a sense of obligation is not caring, it is co-dependence; enabling the other person to settle for less with you using them as an excuse to also not become what you know you are capable of. Often times it is the courage to walk alone that brings forth the companions worthy of your company."

-Neo Blaqness-

WHEN NOT TO

"Paying the price for the pain someone else inflicted is like taking on a baby you didn't have the pleasure to create. You just may have the heart to do it, but some demons are best dealt with by their own masters."

-Neo Blaqness-

HOPE FLOATS

"**S**ometimes a friend will lift you up, not because he is stronger, but because his feet can touch the bottom and he can hold his breath longer. For when your lungs are full of air, you aren't quite as heavy then. Consider, still, that his grows stale, while waiting for you to swim."

-Neo Blaqness-

WALK WITH ME

"The question is never about whether you can accept me for who I am. It's my job to have that settled for myself and within myself. The real question I always ask is, am I a better person for having you in my life? You see life is about CHANGE. Now and tomorrow are two different things. You may well be where I am right now but are you ready for where I am going? Relationships are not about settling down. They are about the JOURNEY. If ass is your path you will be covered in grass just in time for the rest of us to step over you on our way to better things. So don't tell me how good you are at laying it down. I am more interested in how far you can walk." *-Neo Blaqness-*

KNIGHTS AND DAMSELS

"For those who ponder the fate of chivalry and ask, where have all the flowers gone. The flowers of our time blossom differently with age. Be careful when looking for chivalry because such expectations on your part come with certain obligations that may not be worth the flowers. We should give because it is purposed in our heart. Giving is like a voice across a great canyon. When you hear no echo, you know there is no substance on the other side. It isn't that you should expect the echo. Neither is it that you should ignore its absence."

-Neo Blaqness-

AGELESS

"**A** man whose heart is held by the beauty of your spirit, can never be lost to the illusion of age. For the flower of youth lasts only for a season, but the seed of its beauty endures forever."

-Neo Blaqness-

THE LONGING

"I guess I could say that I miss you, but that would be a lie. I just long to hear a voice added to your ever presence."

-Neo Blaqness-

ABUNDANTLY

"A life
without true love
is like
a smile
that no one sees
warmth
without a breeze
a sky
without a sea
of stars
to gaze upon
and dream
a child
without laughter
no hope of
happy ever after
just existing
missing out
embracing

fear and doubt
replacing the
very gift
Christ died
that you might see
that you might love
and live your life
having both
abundantly"

-Neo Blaqness-

BLIND BEAUTY

"**I**f I had no eyes to see you, no hands to touch you, no nose to smell your fragrance, no ears to hear your voice, and no mouth to taste your lips. In the absence of all the things that speak to my senses, if the only thing left to tell me of you was your spirit, who would it say that you are? That is the only person that matters to me, because, in the end, it is that person who matters most to God."

-Neo Blagness-

TIN MAN

" **I** remember an assignment I had once in grade school to write an essay asking a question of anyone in history. Of course I don't recall who I chose, but today I think I would choose the Tin Man from the Wizard of Oz. I would ask him how did it work out for you? That heart thing. Was it worth it?"

-Neo Blaqness-

IN SEASON

"**N**ever apologize for knowing what you want. And stop getting caught up when what somebody else wants isn't you. Sometimes it isn't about somebody being right or wrong, but just wrong for each other at the present. Just be thankful one of you is strong enough to be honest and not ruin a friendship out of guilt or sympathy.

It is too easy, when you actually do love someone, to think you owe them a chance just because they ask. You have heard me say before that a heart that is won is never as valuable as one that is freely given. You shouldn't have to convince anyone to be in a relationship with you. Just be yourself. Know yourself. Trust yourself. And you will draw to you those who are meant to walk this life with you.

Likewise, before the moon gave us tides and the sun gave us seasons, there was a time when both the earth and the moon roamed freely until settling into the order that we now know. The Earth didn't have to rope the moon, and the sun doesn't have to ask the earth to revolve around it. It happened naturally. To everything there is a season, and a time to every purpose under heaven [Ecclesiastes 3:1].

You may not like the climate of your love life right now but your greater concern should be the seeds that you plant. What are you sowing right now that you may later regret having to reap when your life finally begins to blossom?"

-Neo Blaqness-

A SIGHT TO BEHOLD

" **I**f there is one thing I wish I could go back and teach every woman when she was a little girl, it would be the difference between sexy and beauty. A man truly worthy of your sexy will, first know, how to appreciate your beauty. The problem is that most women today struggle to even find the beauty within themselves. Trying to keep a man with your sexy is like trying to feed the hungry with a picture of food."

-Neo Blagness-

GOLD FEVER

"It is very easy to find someone to share your bed. It really isn't that hard to find someone to share your heart. But finding someone worth sharing your life with is the most precious discovery of them all. The problem is that too many people are like treasure hunters. They just can't stop looking for gold even when they have more than what they could spend in a lifetime. We really need to learn to treasure the love that we have already found."

-Neo Blaqness-

OF PEAS AND CARROTS

"The reason loneliness is so painful to endure is because it means waking up each day with your life meaning, seemingly, nothing to no one. Sure God loves you. And family loves you. But in the average person's mind, they don't really count. They kind of had no choice but to be stuck with you. It's like my dislike of peas and carrots. I will never eat them alone but I will if they are drowned in a soup or stew. But that is not love. It is, however, the way many of us end up living and trying to call it love. To be chosen by someone without having to change the core of who you are is the love that makes those lonely peas and carrots happy to be consumed. Just, not by me."

-Neo Blaqness-

LONELINESS

"Loneliness is the over-anticipation of graduation instead of mastering the education and preparation of oneself that can only be learned through times of solitude.**"**

-Neo Blaqness-

A SOLITARY CHOICE

"Loneliness is both an emotion and an action, or in English terms- a subject and a verb. We can be lonely and we can act out of loneliness. We can be lonely surrounded by a hundred or a thousand people. We can be married and still lonely. We can be alone and lonely. But the reasons that we are alone, make a huge difference in how much we can handle the emotion of loneliness. If you are alone because you have made a decision to be alone rather than to compromise your principles, even though you feel lonely, you have made a CHOICE of SOLITUDE. However, acting out of loneliness only seeks to have a void filled by whatever is available that remotely resembles what we want.**"

-Neo Blaqness-

LOVE AND HAPPINESS

" I t is said that one of the definitions of insanity is doing the same thing over and over again and expecting a different result. If that is, indeed, true, then love must be the most common form of insanity. Not only do we seek it out, no matter how many times we are unsuccessful at it, we often repeat the same patterns to fulfill our desires in those with whom we are least likely to truly find happiness."

-Neo Blaqness-

OFF THE HOOK

"**W**hen it comes to relationships, while it is true that there are plenty of fish in the sea, before you start complaining about what you are catching, consider the bait you are using, and where you are dropping your lines. What looks good on the plate don't always taste that good going down."

-Neo Blaqness-

BON APPETIT

"She said she would make a meal out of me if I would eat her alive. But I told her I didn't have much of an appetite for just desserts."

-Neo Blaqness-

SEBASTIAN

"**W**hen using your body as bait, you must remember, after the fish dun ate, his instinct is to stay offa da plate."

-Neo Blaqness-

YIPPEE KI YAY

"Old hoes neva die, dey just sag off into da bedroom."

-Neo Blaqness-

L–O–V–E

"**W**hen a woman exclaims what she wants a man to do to her, there is but one four letter word that excites and impresses me."

-Neo Blaqness-

LOOKING

"I would rather gaze upon your heart than peep beneath your panties.**"**

-Neo Blaqness-

THIS SIDE UP

" **I**f you want to stop having problems finding someone on your level, you can start by not bending over ass up scraping the bottom of the barrel."

-Neo Blaqness-

BACKSTROKE

"A man that you land on your back will eventually take flight when clouds roll in or whenever the coast is clear."

-Neo Blaqness-

SIGNALS

"When you tell someone you want some company, you are talking with your body. When you say you would like companionship, you are speaking from your heart."

-Neo Blaqness-

OH MAH PEOPLE

"**M**y kingdom for a black woman who is NOT stuck on her big booty, her cleavage, Patro'n, weed, pretty feet, fake hair, and don't got more pictures on her body than a Scooby Doo coloring book, but is also NOT Aunt Esther from Sanford and Son... OHHHH GLORY!!!"

-Neo Blaqness-

BONDLESS LOVE

"If you are looking for someone that can HANDLE you, then you are looking to be OWNED. If you are looking for someone to RESPECT you, then you are looking to be LOVED."

-Neo Blaqness-

UPSIDE DOWN

"If you got to take out a loan to keep from being alone, you better check the interest rate of your love and re-appraise the perceived value of your relationship."

-Neo Blaqness-

CONUNDRUM

"**S**ometimes I wonder which is easier - for a woman to find a man who won't lie to her? Or for a man to find a woman who can stop lying to herself."

-Neo Blaqness-

TRAFFIC JAM

"Some compromises you make to try to hold on to someone hell bent on walking away, can damage the chances of meeting that someone, who always intended to stay.**"**

-Neo Blaqness-

PROVERBS

"A man will usually hold to his word only as often as a woman holds to her virtue. Seduction is the lure for liars and the vocation of vice, while modesty unveils the motive of a man, and prevails upon his passions a lust to know her in spirit and in truth.**"**

-Neo Blaqness-

BLAQFUSCIUS

"**B**laqFuscius say: May ur woman's heart be bigger than her azz and ur man's patience be longer than his penis."

-Neo Blaqness-

MATCH GAME

"I used to play with matches, until I came to understand that, just because you blow off an old flame and toss it in the garbage, don't mean it's gone completely out, or can't be reignited by something else you forgot you threw in there that can burn down your house."

-Neo Blaqness-

SKEERED

"**O**nly a love built or sustained on lies, fears its own demise."

-Neo Blaqness-

PARITY

"A wise woman will help a stallion to run his race instead of feeding a mule who will never pull a plow. And a wise man looks for a woman who can pull more weight than she gains from the food she eats.**"**

-Neo Blaqness-

THIRD FINGER

"I asked her when her husband was coming home? She said HE hadn't decided yet. I asked her how she felt about that? She said SHE hadn't decided yet. She asked me if I thought they were on their way to divorce? I said I hadn't decided if they were actually married yet.**"**

-Neo Blaqness-

MAN IN THE MIRROR

"When someone stares you in the face and says I love you, sometimes they aren't speaking to you, but to the reflection of them self in the pupils of your eyes."

-Neo Blaqness-

MIRROR MIRROR

" If you wake up in the morning and cannot find a reason to smile when you look in the mirror, your reflection is trying to tell you something that your heart has already known for far too long. "

-Neo Blaqness-

EMPTY

"Like the sounds of the sea from an empty shell, so too can you hear the echo of tears when placing your head upon the breast of a hollow heart."

-Neo Blagness-

LYING WONDER

"The problem with lying to the person you love is that it makes them wonder how much of your love might also be a lie."

-Neo Blaqness-

BOTTOMLESS

"**B**efore you accuse someone of loving you less, you should first check for holes in the bottom of your heart."

-*Neo Blaqness*-

BRICK LAYERS

"The promises you break to the heart of the one you vowed to love, become the bricks that build the wall between you and God, and the oven that eventually burns you in the hell of your own creation."

-Neo Blaqness-

GOT IT HONEST

"What if...someone once held you as a baby, in the same way you now act when you hold another person's heart? Who knows? ...perhaps they did."

-Neo Blaqness-

FREE AT LAST

"**H**ad I not loved you, I would have never known such pain; nor the utter joy of freedom that your absence has taught me to embrace. We are often the prison, the warden, and the parole board of our own choices. As for yours, I no longer choose to be a member of that jury."

-Neo Blaqness-

WHEN LOVE FAILS

"Someone once asked me, all things being equal, who's at fault when love falls apart? It is usually the lies men say to the face, and the ones women speak to the heart.**"**

-Neo Blaqness-

FACE FIRST

"Sometimes you just want to love so bad that you actually fall on purpose just to test your faith that someone will catch you. Funny thing is, smacking the ground face first isn't enough to stop you from doing it again. I can only conclude, then, that love is the purpose of living and that, by avoiding the fall, we are already dead.**"**

-Neo Blaqness-

PRIORITIES & OPTIONS

"**L**ove is not about priorities and options. It is about respect. Some of us are more needy than others. And others of us prefer not to be smothered. The key is to make certain that BEFORE you decide to commit to someone, that the same things that are important to you are important to the other person. Little choices amount to big differences in priorities that can really destroy a relationship.

Most people are generally consistent with their priorities. When we feel like we have been burned and treated as an option, normally it is because we made changing the other person our priority instead of exercising the option to respect what was clearly in front of us."

-Neo Blaqness-

MASQUERADE

"It is very easy to lose yourself when trying to become a reflection of someone else's desire. People who live a masquerade life often forget how hot and labor-some a breath can be even while others applaud the costume. Eventually, the true face must be revealed to those who may have spoken to you differently or even not at all, had they known it was you under the mask."

-Neo Blaqness-

IT TAKES A FOOL

"Love is an instrument- a tool. It doesn't care about how it is used. Just like the old saying, guns don't kill people- people kill people. A lot of times we play around with love like a loaded weapon. We don't mean to pull the trigger or to harm anybody, but we fail to respect the damage it can do when held in undisciplined hands.

Love will let you love anybody. Love will let you compromise everything you believe in. Love will let you make a fool of yourself. Love will let you love somebody more than you love yourself. Love will let you get beat up within an inch of your life. Love will let you believe your life is not worth living without a certain person. Love will let you give up your whole life so somebody can live off your work. Just like a gun can be used for justice or for murder- love loves nothing about how you use it; and love don't love nobody. It is only about how and why you CHOOSE to use love that makes the USE of love something that is good or bad.

Do you hijack people with love? Do you rob people with love? Do you make people guilty with love? Do you smother people with love? How much time do you practice loving yourself before trying it on others? And what are your rules of engagement? Are your standards for giving love the same as your standards for receiving it? And if that is, indeed, the case, then why are you having problems with love? It's a perfectly good tool when used in the right hands.

You see the reason it takes a fool to learn that love don't love nobody is because we keep fooling ourselves into believing the problem with love is everybody but the person we are looking at in the mirror. We get into relationships and hand out love like a loaded weapon to a two year old then wonder how we got shot. Don't blame the bullet. Don't blame the gun. Don't blame the person with the poor aim. The moment you see love being mishandled or taken for granted and fail to check your judgment or the qualification of the other person, love will make it do what it do- and like a stray bullet at a drive by shooting, it will, sooner or later, take someone out."

-Neo Blaqness-

FLO WITH IT

"**G**oing with the flow is the lowest form of commitment. Even lower than casual sex because you could end up investing much more than your body with no obligation that the other party be responsible.

Do not mistake a strong sense of direction as moving too fast. It is, more often, a sign of maturity- sometimes too mature for you. So instead of going with the flow, perhaps it is best to consider someone more your speed. Also, that fabulous ship with no engine you are considering hopping aboard, could take you on a destination cruise that is not quite the adventure you had in mind."

-Neo Blaqness-

OF WOMEN AND MEN

"A woman under 30
is still learning
to find herself.
A woman over 30
is just starting
to trust herself.
A woman in her 40s
has finally begun
to love herself.
A woman in her 50s
is confident enough
to be herself.
A woman in her 60s
seeks to give
of herself
A man under 30
already thinks
he is a man.
A man in his 30s

defines manhood
by things
A man over 40
defines manhood
by accomplishments
A man over 50
begins to think
about his legacy
A man over 60
finally
understands love."

-Neo Blaqness-

ONLY FOR NOW

"I don't know every answer
Each day brings more questions
Each experience new wisdom
that redefines
what I thought
I already knew
So I am only as sure
as I can be today
tomorrow may show me
another way
like a child
food despised
and left uneaten
now mature in mind
not taking for granted
the nourishment needed
I sup from the cup of life
as bitter as
oft times sweet

I vomit not
for its something to eat
lest I starve of no wisdom
grow fat
from meaningless treats
So sedentary in my ways
I can no longer see my feet
progress halted
my stride and my gait
would fail me
lest I exercise my mind
To run a path
is not always to know
the destination
To describe the journey
is not always to know
where you are
But to know
where you have been
is to know
how far you've come
only
for now"

-Neo Blaqness-

FAITH WALK

"Walk by faith
not by sight
cuz when your spirit
tells you
something's
not right
yet you follow
your eyes
into the night
thinking the path
to Heaven
is between
some thighs
and find
the devil
in disguise
and a million
reasons to start
to cry

and your mind tells you
you want to die
all you need do
is close your eyes
and walk the path
you can't deny
you somehow already
knew by heart
the evidence of faith
is the well trodden road
beneath your feet
made by others
who walked out
from the dark"

-Neo Blaqness-

BEATS AND MEASURES

" In my life I have found that many things beyond my understanding were simply beyond my time, and that the misunderstandings I have had with others were merely beyond there's.

But when, we who are the instruments, yield to the baton of The Conductor, we find there to be a grand orchestration at work with us each counting the beats and measures in anticipation of our time to emerge in this symphony of life.

Sometimes the timpani, other times the strings, still others the trumpet. By solo or section we all play our part. The noise, which is often our life, is only our instruments warming up before the tap tap tap of God, calls us to face the music."

-Neo Blagness-

IN DIGESTION

"Sometimes slow digestion
will cause you to question
what you been eatin and when
Don't mistake contemplation
for constipation
and worry about
what's not coming out
of the other end
or equate
that because you salivate
means it's something
you should always taste
for the more things nutritious
you ingest in your life
the less
your body
will waste"

-Neo Blaqness-

NO NEVER ALONE

" **L**oneliness is not always as self-ish as a desire to have someone love us, but rather that we also have within us, a love that burns to be shared. It is the very reason that we were created, that we have been redeemed, and that we suffer the foolishness of one another rather than live a solitary life.

It is, perhaps, the noblest character of man, that we should continue to desire to share love despite our abuse of the same when we receive it. In this we are, indeed, the proverbial fallen fruits of our father tho- not so far from the tree in that we continue to share our love for the very same reasons that we yet live.

Solitude is like a necessary sleep that we must have at times in order to balance our spirit. But when solitude becomes an endless aloneness, it is a depressive rest that seeks not to regenerate in order to live, but to lay in wasteful defeat and await only the end.

And this is why the Creator of all things said, it is not good that man should be alone. When a widow dies so soon after the loss of her mate, it is not so much that she misses his love, tho surely she does, but when there is no longer a place for her love in this world, time is of no more use to her.

I have learned that a place FOR love is infinitely more important in life than an individual face TO love. But when we confuse loneliness as a need to find that FACE instead of asking to be led to that PLACE that needs our love, that is when we suffer the most abuse of our love, and often at the hand of our desperate choices.

Sometimes we are fortunate to have both the face and place dwell in an individual. And there is nothing wrong with having such a desire. But in the absence of both, do not trap yourself in aloneness when there are so many unfilled cracks and crevices of love throughout this world that could use the goodness of a willing heart.

You may feel as though you do not have a lot to give, but a single spark of light is as brilliant as a sun to the eyes of those who dwell in darkness. Just be God's light... and you will never be alone."

-Neo Blagness-

EYES WIDE SHUT

"There is a joy I try to live by, and that I endeavor to share with every soul I have been blessed to encounter. To try to be, at least, that one human being to understand the reasons for the absence of joy in the life of another. To shine some gladness over sadness so it can see its way out of the deep. For as anyone who has ever known darkness understands, it takes only a speck of light to show the way. What light I have, I give gladly. But sadly, I have found it cannot pierce the darkness of closed eyes."

-Neo Blaqness-

NO REGRETS

"I used to regret the time I wasted on those who took my kindness or my love for granted. Those who knowingly used me with no intention of being honorable, and who walk the street as though the hurt they have left in their wake is of no concern to them, and it would anger me to see the stupid smile I felt they had no right to have on their face.

But I came to understand, that if my kindness or love was truly the gift that I intended it to be, then I could not put a price on it and hold it over the head of another for what they chose to do with it.

My heart was reminded of the days walking down the streets of Baltimore with a friend who scolded me as I gave some change to a homeless person. He said "that man is a drunk and you know what he will do with it".

And I replied, "that may be so but my spirit told me to give it to him. The rest is between him and God". When I started to apply the same principle to those who have hurt my heart, I soon found the peace that I truly hope that they too, might someday discover."

—Neo Blaqness—

AUTUMN

"I get excited when August comes because I know autumn will soon be upon us. People often ask me what is it that I find so appealing about autumn? Is it the color of the leaves? The briskness of the air? The grey cloudy skies? The coming of the winter snow? They all point to the outward expressions of the season.

With the exception of the holidays, I hear so many say, at summer's end, that they would gladly flock to the warmer skies of the south if they could. But not me.

To me, autumn is a metaphor for life. It requires of us an accounting of what we have done with our more blessed days. Plants humbly say goodbye to their outer beauty, knowing what is necessary to survive, and anticipating a shortness of warmth and sun, they prepare to live off of the depth of their roots where the water remains un-frozen; held by an earth that is warm from its core.

Likewise I have found that many, who least enjoy the coming of winter, are not so fortunately rooted in the comforts of love, nor the layers of a blanket's embrace that snuggles against a mind's introspection as it contemplates the blossoms of the coming spring.

Each year, I gladly give up a host of sun-ny days for the infinite wisdom that the seeds of autumn yield to my soul."

-Neo Blaqness-

OLD SOULS

"I have always known my soul to be much older than the time I have lived in this place. That the spirit which manifests within this body is but a projection of the light visible to the naked eye; separated by the prism which is the veil between the finite now and eternity.

And as the ozone protects our human life from the greatness of the sun, so too does such a veil protect us from the madness of all knowledge. For if what little I know already consumes and requires so much of my small life, I am humbled at the thought of what existence I must evolve into and embody, that is capable of holding and withstanding the great weight of responsibility that must surely come with the answers to all things.**"**

-Neo Blaqness-

SOUL FOOD

"In many ways, I have never considered myself an ordinary man. Neither am I an extraordinary one.

We are all born with the basic ingredients of life. How sweet a confection, how rich to the taste, how fulfilling to the soul we are is really a matter of what we make of it.

Some of us serve up our lives as fast food to drive through relationships. Others as culinary delights to the fastidious tastes of the high minded. Indeed, I have been all of those things.

But what has fancied my spirit best, has been the mmm mmm good of becoming the warm comfort food upon the smiling palates of those whose hearts are in need of a reminder of home."

-Neo Blaqness-

GOD'S GALLEY

"**L**ike everyone else, I used to say I just wanted to be loved by someone. But then I realized that if God couldn't convince me of His love, and I couldn't convince me that I was worthy of loving even myself, how could I truly recognize the genuine love of another?

Love is not unlike the difference between fine dining and home cooking. We fancy ourselves as something more from eating the best cuts served by a master chef but often leave such restaurants barely full with our pockets empty.

And yet a meal made from what you could afford to keep in your cabinets, satisfies the hunger and warms the heart without being the poorer for it. Others may seek to wine and dine as compensation for what they lack within. I, however, have discovered that, within the galley of my heart, is stocked the finest of God's ingredients with which to bake a home cooked love."

-Neo Blaqness-

HONGRY

"**S**um of yall treat friendship like a pot luck dinner. Show up wit a car fulla chillun and a dollar sto bag wit nuttin but styrofoam cups and aluminum foil talkin bout yall hongry."

-Neo Blaqness-

YO AZZ BETTA EAT

"They say if you love something set it free; if it comes back to you, it was meant to be. Aiight, well I do understand dat part, but da troof is dat if it don't come back it prolly on somebody else dinner plate."

—Neo Blaqness—

ALACARTE'

" I have learned that not everyone who claims to be hungry is starving. You can't pick your meals when asking for a handout. **"**

-Neo Blaqness-

WAIST NOT

"The world would be a much better place if those who won't act their age, at least, acted the size of their waist."

-Neo Blaqness-

LOAN CARE

" I need to stop lending out my GivaDamn cuz yall always sending it back broke..."

-Neo Blaqness-

LATE PAYMENTS

"I don't care how broke you are or how messed up your credit is. We all have stuff we go through. But, out of all the debt or bills you might have, the one thing I am going to check to see if you pay more than anything, is ATTENTION.**"**

-Neo Blaqness-

GENDER NEUTRAL

"I don't care about your sexuality. I care about your humanity. Assholes come in all genders."

-Neo Blaqness-

HELL NO

"**N**o, I never told you to go to Hell, all I said is that Satan called and said you forgot your tooth-brush."

-Neo Blaqness-

A THIN LINE

> **"I** never measure my life by how many people love me or hate me, but whether or not I can live with their reasons for either one.**"**

-Neo Blaqness-

THE CALL

"**L**ife calls us all to greatness. Some before many. Many to only one. The thought of living up to either calling, humbles me equally."

-Neo Blaqness-

EXPECTING

" **I** have never tried to live up to any-one's expectations of me. That would be a step down from the ones I already have for myself."

-Neo Blaqness-

NON-PROPHET

"If the truth means I never make another dime in my life, then I shall gladly forfeit Caesar's riches for the poverty of God's."

-Neo Blaqness-

TO STAND

"To stand for anything
you believe is right
is not about hatred
it's not about might
it's not about proving
who's wrong or who's right
it's not about
everything being
black or white
but about what stirs
within your soul
that you can live with
when your eyes grow old
and can clearly see
that you tried to be wise
despite the temptation
to compromise
which is not alone
a dirty word

when it's made from things
you've truly learned
and not just
changing your mind
in some feeble attempt
to buy more time
to figure out a way
to have what you want
but never really change
to stand alone
on the highway of life
in a mist of gray
with everyone driving
recklessly about
while you somehow
know the way
is no miracle
or arrogance
that you arrive unscathed
some see only the fog
others trust the light
to lead them on
their way"

-Neo Blaqness-

THE PATH

"Always choose to be who you are.
until wisdom calls you to change
Some are meant to walk with you far
whilst others may think you strange
But the biggest mistake
that you can make
is to change
just so you can fit in
Neither stubbornly
stay in one place
but that your reasons
should come from within
For everyone has
a direction in life
a path, a purpose, a pace
Destiny is not about
finishing first
but simply running the race
Not for the cheers

neither for fear
of leaving another behind
The true measure of faith
is not just in our walk
but the paths
we leave others
to find"

-Neo Blaqness-

DANCE TO THE MUSIC

" I suppose if we pay too close attention to the music of our lives, there wouldn't be much left to dance to- unless, of course, we do the unthinkable... and begin to listen to the true music within."

-Neo Blagness-

A DIFFERENT DRUM

"This sin I embrace whole-heartedly. If in the condemnation of my heart must I dwell on the outskirts of acceptance, I shall greet you there- each and every one of you; that we may, together, turn this hell, into the paradise that only such hearts are able to create."

-Neo Blaqness-

TO THINE OWN SELF

"**B**eing true to yourself is a lot like giving in to the music of life and just dancing as if no one else is watching to a rhythm that only you can hear. At first, others may think you have gone mad. But after watching your feet, the beat of the unheard drum becomes clear by the sound of your toes lifting your soles to the sky and your hands waving from the air as your spirit takes flight. Each leap lasting merely seconds leaving deep footprints of joy in the sands of time, whilst others contemplate whether to laugh, or likewise dance."

-Neo Blaqness-

WITH THESE HANDS

"**D**ignity is the respect you maintain for yourself even when others show you none. It is a conscious awareness that your everyday walk and talk either feeds or kills the lies told about you, or puts to rest those things of the past that may even have been true.

In my life I have found the face of dignity not so much possessing lips of eloquence, but, more often, weary eyes and calloused hands."

-Neo Blaqness-

ORDINARY PEOPLE

"**A**ny man who fancies himself as extraordinary, arrogantly denies the power of the Creator who has placed greatness within us all, and favors not one above the other, but increases both blessing and wisdom upon those who remain faithful in the face of adversity and fear.

For how much greater is the hero than the workman who makes the shield which protects his life, or the miner who digs to find the workman's ore? In all these things there is honor, without which the hero would fall and the enemy prevail.

Test not the faithfulness of God by dwelling upon His grace. That Goliath fell at the hand a single boy with a slingshot and stone forgives not the cowardice of those who trembled in the face of a giant.

For how much more extraordinary a testimony is there that the ordinary stand as one, than for one to stand up for many?"

-Neo Blaqness-

SING CHOIRS OF ANGELS

"**A**n evil voice may bellow its baritone from the depths of hate and shake the earth, but when the chorus of the righteous fills the air, it echoes and reverberates from Heaven, comforting the soul.

As our ancestors sang from the cotton fields of their captivity, so too must we find our voice in the growing chorus against the killing fields and injustices of our time."

-Neo Blaqness-

KUNTA KINTE

"What do we do when we get a dog? We give it a name. And we call it that name over and over again until it has no choice but to respond, or not enjoy the comforts of being owned."

-Neo Blaqness-

CRABS IN A BARREL

"**H**aving entered the age of our greatest liberties, we must be careful that the ties that so importantly bound us one to another through the storms of discrimination, do not now sink us as the waters rise. We must no longer be beggars at the feet of assimilation, but leaders at the seat of self determination."

-Neo Blaqness-

HUE MAN

" I have learned that the battle to be won is not based on the dominant color of one's skin- which is not a reliable basis of indignation; but rather the unequivocal hue of the heart. A dark soul wears many outer shades."

-Neo Blaqness-

BLACKLASH

"**A**merica has a political fixation of fear of "blacklash". A black candidate for anything is measured by one prevailing question that is on the mind of every middle-aged or older white person who votes. This question is not always a conscious or direct one. It is often exposed by the way white people examine closely every aspect of everything socially or politically discoverable about a black candidate. The question boils down to How p****d off is he or she about slavery and being black in America? The fear of that singular issue is the litmus test upon which a black person is trusted with power in America."

-Neo Blaqness-

RECALCULATING

"The true lesson of the solidarity between black and white, that could only have made possible the election of a black president, is that, like the end of all major battles, we must now stand down to emerge into a diversity of cause. Otherwise we have battled only to prove the point of the defeated. That it is them; or us- and we give form to myth- out of which fear creates a more desperate enemy."

-Neo Blaqness-

GOD SHED HIS GRACE

"For those of us who endeavor to walk in the light, the choice we value most is not that of vengeance, but that there is often more to gain through mercy. Of all the lessons learned by the decedents of former slaves, this is the one from which America has benefited most."

-Neo Blaqness-

A BRUTHA'S COLORS

" I love God above all else. I know I fail to show it everyday as much as I should. What is important to me, as should be to you, is that if you believe your cultural manifestation of loving and living for God is true, then you should accept anyone who is willing to live with you by that spiritual standard of commitment. A true sellout must also be an infidel to someone else's God. Not many are willing or ready to suffer that wrath. Those who do, should be counted as no less than brethren."

-Neo Blaqness-

JOSEPH'S COAT

"**W**hen the fabric of our being is woven from these spinning wheels of words, what will the tapestry reveal as to who we really are? Bitter and ugly? Or victorious and magnificent? I challenge each of you to weave the latter."

-Neo Blaqness-

BLAQNESS

"I love my life for what I have been blessed to learn and what I have been humbled to be able to give to others. It's not much, but hopefully enough to fulfill my purpose for being here. Which is not to be black; but, as best I can, to be Godly. Blackness just helps me get there a little faster.**"**

-Neo Blaqness-

BLACKONOMICS

"**D**espite the cold, reckless, and, oft times, ruthlessness of capitalism, black mamas have always taken heed to that old Christian axiom of, what does it profit a man to gain the whole world yet lose his own soul.

There is a hymn to the heart of blackness that makes little sense to the rest of the business world. It is a composition of compassion written for the voices of a chorus. It runs contrary to the monetary melody that seeks to satisfy only the soul of the soloists.

To forgo the herald of trumpets only to be a voice among many is a modesty seen as an affront to capital gain. And yet, the unbridled larceny of the American spirit remains a self-inflicting wound that reopens now and then to remind us of our responsibility one to another. Except for black folk, it isn't something that needs reminding. It is something that is daily lived."

-Neo Blaqness-

PREJUDICE

"We are each prejudiced by experience, whilst some of us are taught that way. But some matters are just too serious, to let bigotry seize the day."

-Neo Blagness-

THE VICTOR

"It is the destiny of the defeated to either dedicate themselves to the divine or devote themselves to the will of their temporary master.

Providence will always speak more eloquently of the faithful than of those whom would call themselves the victor. For a man who would seek to prove himself the superior at the conquering of another, has truly revealed his worth as nothing at all."

-Neo Blaqness-

THE COUNT

"**M**ost people don't realize that tomorrow is not promised until they have a reason to count the days until they will be gone or the days that they have missed someone they hoped to have had in their life a longer time. I'm not just talking about death. There can be many reasons that days can pass us by.

A common mistake we make in life is allowing our past pains to cause us to fear the now and keep us from seizing the opportunities of today. I would rather fail in the trying than to simply live in the denying myself a chance at something good out of fear.

At least, that is what I tell myself, just before I get back on my feet, after those eternity of seconds pass that come in the life of

every fighter, in which he sometimes contemplates, just staying down."

-Neo Blaqness-

HARK THE HERALD

"That anything in life should ever bring you to your knees is no sign of weakness, but of opportunity. Consider that a sprinter must kneel before a fast race, a jumper must also bend before a great leap, and a strong man begins a heavy lift from his legs.

Our knees provide the momentum for our greatest feats. Our knees are the point of power from which we spring forward with the strength to push beyond, to rise above, and to uplift. They were never designed to remain on the ground, but only to serve as the herald of action."

-Neo Blaqness-

DO THE MATH

"Sometimes bad circumstances may give you the illusion that you are only a fraction of yourself; especially when life seems a little top heavy.

Remember there is often a wholeness to be found by simply dividing the numerator by the denominator; making the remaining problems much more manageable.**"**

-Neo Blaqness-

SUCCESS AND LUCK

" It is often said that both success and luck come from the same place. It is simply where preparation meets opportunity. Whether it is on a job or in a relationship, how prepared are you to meet the opportunities that each present? Do you stay up late or out drinking knowing you get to go to work? Do you still act like you're living this life alone even though you have somebody in it you're supposed to be in a relationship with?

Success is usually the opportunities we take for ourselves. Luck is the opportunities that see us coming. I would rather be successful than lucky. At least I know the motive behind the opportunity.

People who consider themselves lucky are indebted to whoever brings them luck. If you consider yourself lucky to have your job or lucky to have someone in your life, you may well be qualified to have both of those things. But you entered into those relationships on the terms of the person who hired you or accepted you.

Therefore a lucky person is not equal in value to the person who provides the opportunity. Which is why I never wish anyone good luck. That is nothing more than hoping they become a well paid slave.

A successful person understands his or her value coming in and is prepared to maximize it with any opportunity they see. When they feel undervalued, they are prepared to listen, learn, grow, fight, or move on in order to be successful- constantly challenging themselves to evolve to the next level.

Ultimately success is never about wealth of things, but wealth of values.

What do you value? Who do you value? And why do you value?

When you prepare around a set of values that you are willing to live with, you usually attract opportunities of similar or matching values. That is why the most successful of people always do what they love the most, and not what they feel will make them the most money. Everything else just comes with the territory."

-Neo Blaqness-

NEEDLESS

"In my youth I often struggled between knowing the truth of my needs and the selfishness of my desires, until I realized that the evidence that I have never truly suffered need, rests in the fact that I am still very much alive."

-Neo Blaqness-

A CORONATION

"Our greatest enemy in life is, none other than, our own choices. Not the choices that lead to mistakes, because that is a part of our living, but the choice to not learn from them. That is the real difference between pain and agony, and weariness and exhaustion.

Weariness glories in wisdom which is a light of hope that restores one's strength, while stubbornness battles to exhaustion- a darkened decision to fight with a point rather than a sword of truth.

Wisdom finds meaning in pain, choosing to grow from it, and stubbornness finds purpose in agony, choosing to live in it.

A Crown of Glory is promised to the dead who have chosen the path of Christ. But a Crown of Life has been promised to the living who have chosen a path of wisdom. Too many of us are wearing our crowns in the wrong order."

-Neo Blaqness-

ALL IN THE ASKING

"There is no such thing as unanswered prayer, only undesired answers. For within every travail lay opportunity, and in every opportunity a choice, and within each choice there is right and wrong according to that which we know and in whom we place our faith.

Therefore, in equal measure to the substance of our prayers, should we, foremost, ask for understanding of our circumstances.

For what profit you to pray for sanctuary from the cold and the Father give you wood and you burn it and die, lest you receive also the understanding to build a shelter from the wind that could quench the fire whilst you sleep?"

-Neo Blaqness-

A FIERY DOVE

"Don't be out here blaming God when you are too busy to recognize the blessings right in front of you or when you keeping running right back into the fires he led you out of.

There is an old saying that you can't stop the birds from flying over you but you sure can keep them from making a nest on your head. Just what are you letting *nest* inside of you?"

-Neo Blaqness-

BY AND BY

"I never sorrow over things for which I can do nothing but pray. For it is in those moments that I am most comforted that the result will be exactly as it should, tho it may take time for my heart and mind to understand."

-Neo Blaqness-

FIRST

"**B**eing first means nothing if you move so fast that you have no idea how to get back. That is why those who aspire to greatness are the least qualified to lead. But those who walk humbly in the counsel of wisdom, leave a path worthy to be followed."

-Neo Blaqness-

CORINTHIAN GLASS

"The glass darkly no longer waits for perfection to come, only for someone to light up the lens."

-*Neo Blaqness*-

PAST PROLOGUE

(Paraphrasing Mathew)

"**W**hen an unclean spirit comes out of a person, it roams through dry places looking for rest but doesn't find any. So it says, 'I'll go back to my house that I came from.' And when it finds the house vacant, swept, and put in order, it goes and brings with it seven other spirits more evil than itself, and they enter and settle down there."

ONE MORAL OF THE STORY

"Be mindful of the company you keep, and the things you are likely to repeat, when deciding to live in the past."

-Neo Blaqness-

MOTES AND BEAMS

"She said to me, you know what they out there saying about me so why are you so good to me when all they gonna say is I slept with you for favors?

And I replied, because God has been good to me in spite of myself. He is not ashamed to call me His own so why should I deny your friendship when I don't even deserve His?"

-Neo Blaqness-

DEBT FREE

"I pulled him aside and asked, why do you let them treat you that way? He replied that they led him to Christ and he felt like he owed a debt from his days wasted as an alcoholic.

And so I said, Jesus paid it all my friend- when they led you to Him they neglected to tell you your debt was canceled."

-Neo Blaqness-

AMEN CORNER

" I thought about sinning today, but I don't know how to begin. For there's no space between where your morality starts, and where your hypocrisy ends."

-Neo Blaqness-

CLOSED

"Closed hearts
Closed eyes
Closed ears
Closed minds
Cost souls
Cost lives
Leaves holes
in the wisdom
of time"

-Neo Blaqness-

PONTIUS PEOPLE

"Inhale
Exhale
Pass
Fail
Go to jail
Please us
or Jesus
or
If you must
Fade to dust
Walk alone
or ride
Our bus
Chompin
Stompin
Don't forget
your offerin
Kneel down
to our sound

and receive
your
thorny crown"

-Neo Blaqness-

A QUESTION OF FAITH

"**W**hy do we read scripture as though thousands of years have taught us nothing better than the people in it knew?

They were children compared to what man has discovered about himself and the universe. These discoveries are not a threat to God because we were exhorted to test all things and to take dominion over this realm.

This means taking the time to understand the science and design of the universe so that we will ultimately have no choice but to conclude that there has to be an intentional purpose to it all.

So many things that were a mystery to the primitive understanding of early worshipers that they simply called "God", is what science has discovered to be by intricate design.

It is no threat to God that we have sought such answers, but a testament to the greatness of his handiwork and the fact that we were created to learn all of these mysteries.

If you truly believe that we are made in God's image and that we are the "sons" of God, then aren't the infants who are born of parents taught by their parents in order to someday assume the responsibilities of adulthood?

Thus, as spiritual beings- sons of God made in His image, what are we learning to grow up to be? Dare we admit that the logic reveals that, we ourselves, are gods in training?"

-Neo Blaqness-

FAITH EVOLUTION

"**D**o not mistake religion for personal faith nor written doctrine for living discernment.

We are all victims of societal programming and there comes a point where we who know there is no Santa Clause must disengage from the fraud even if it means departing from those who find life more agreeable remaining therein. We are, in reality, choosing to live in the restoration of what was always meant to be.

The rest are not unlike a band of sentient apes of unlimited potential finding every reason to remain among the trees. Because they refuse to fathom the emancipation of their potential, their enslaved minds only know what those who provide the bananas teach them is safe to think and to explore.

The deck is too well stacked to reason with the greater majority of them. There is much for them to lose compared to the creature comforts of their captivity. All we can do is live, lead, and suffer long in the example of our convictions."

-Neo Blaqness-

ANIMUS LIBERTUS
THE COURAGE TO BE FREE

"**W**hile every generation has a responsibility to learn from the past, we cannot merely be followers of the paths set by those before us. We must find within ourselves a greater wisdom, a more compassionate understanding, and a mind capable of being loosed from all that we think is right, and embrace the courage to challenge all that we have been taught to believe as true.

Because so much history is full of only the interpretations of the day or lies for the comfort of some and the enslavement of others, we cannot merely be satisfied, complacent, or complicit in the bondage of our spirits to that which we cannot also be entrusted to challenge, without, we ourselves, being called less than honorable or spiritual.

We are taught so many things that, somehow, do not seem quite right to us but we fail to question them because the lessons come from those whom we believe love us and always had our best interest at heart.

But if one was born and raised in bondage, what do they know of liberty?

That is why each generation, out of the obscurity of first hand knowledge of bondage must find it's own way of living free from it by creating new paths that will never again lead back to it.

We can no longer believe things just because our parents believed it. Practice things just because our parents practiced it. Live certain ways just because our parents lived it. Were that the purpose of life, women would be footstools and children seen and not heard.

It is not to say that all lessons of the past should be tossed aside with reckless abandon. It is to say that each successive generation enjoys the luxury of perspective absent the bias upon which many traditions are formed.

Man is a spiritual being and religion has nothing to do with spirituality. Religion is man's attempt at a comfortable understanding of himself and his relationship with God.

Spirituality, however, requires that we are never comfortable, that we are always questioning, and striving, and daring to be, and to become, and to grow in boundless ways.

I have found few people willing to pay the price for such freedom when they can settle for a comfortable bondage at a discount.

For some it is simpler to believe in a book and an interpretation than to have the courage to write their own future across the pages of time.

But we each have a responsibility to be of good courage, and to fulfill what our hearts speak to us.

Life is our vessel and enlightenment our sails. Our free will sets the course and challenging traditions gives us insight to the direction before us. We ignore these challenges to our own peril. Nevertheless, it is ours to ignore.

There is nothing sacred to the human experience. No history that is of greater or lesser importance- only knowledge to be gained and wisdom to be gleaned.

I don't want to live and die the way that those before me have. I find contentment in the struggle to discover, than to merely be acceptable by resting in what has already been found.

If nothing more, my children will have something that most never attain- a greater understanding of what the world means to he who fathered them, as I have, likewise, attempted to attain the same of He who created me."

-Neo Blaqness-

REGENESIS

"I do nothing with malevolence of mind, neither to heap weight upon the megalomania by which we canonize living and enslave our minds to sacred books and traditions, and with stagnate hearts persecute progress.

For the rock of my salvation- even for all, is more than a single stone that the builders of such a naive and narrow view of Heaven rejected.

We are all Simone Bar-Jona "the little rocks"- pebbles of the light and truth ignited by our choices; guided, not by an intercessor, but comforted by a spirit within.

Tho humanity is an oft un-tranquil stormy sea of sadness, sin and choice are the pebbles that break the waters, form the lands, and create the foundation of who we are.

That we divide by shape or color or "weight" of beliefs is part of the mosaic created as the waters recede and remove the shifting sands.

We are then given a season to study the picture we create. We rest exposed to the elements, chiseled and worn by the winds of time; with new edges formed while others are reshaped and rounded, preparing for the water's rise where we are reshuffled into our new fit.

The cycle continues until we are so weathered that, we ourselves, become a part of the sands of time giving way to the next pebbles of truth who have rested beneath us - until we are all, ultimately and irrevocably, sand- a cosmic dust infused with the light of generations to become that star worthy to give birth to a new generation of life within the universe. Where we then say, as we once read of the almighties, "let us make in our own image".

Wherein it all begins anew with love- a love of life, and of living, and of progress, and for each other." *-Neo Blaqness-*

EPIPHANY

"There are many gods
but one Creator.
The fear of gods
is the sustenance
of ignorance.
The worship of gods
is the suppression
of truth.
The wisdom of gods
is the perfecting
of our faith.
To walk with gods
is the promise
of our progress.
To be god with gods
is the fulfillment
of our inheritance.
To know this truth
is to honor

the Creator
who is the father
of all gods
big and small.
For we can only make things
out of that
which He created.
The Creator
creates out of love
gods make things
out of vanity
In their image
they fancy the reflection
of themselves
Hidden behind
the darkened glass
of religious mirrors
Until the Creator
reveals them
For the foolishness
of their ways
And welcomes
all that is His
Into the

Fellowship of Spirit
For all souls
Have been made
by His hand
Or through the handiwork
of His design
So worship not
our brothers
Who masquerade
as our fathers
Seeking honor for the seeds
which He created
Their wisdom
and their wickedness
Is for our learning
And our learning
For their edification
For this cycle of life
Is but a single step
Within a greater
Circle of Truth"

-Neo Blaqness-

www.ingramcontent.com/pod-product-compliance
Lightning Source LLC
LaVergne TN
LVHW011419080426
835512LV00005B/149